D1238098

NAVIGATION AND SIGNALING

ELITE FORCES SURVIVAL GUIDE SERIES

Elite Survival
Survive in the Desert with the French Foreign Legion
Survive in the Arctic with the Royal Marine Commandos
Survive in the Mountains with the U.S. Rangers and Army
  Mountain Division
Survive in the Jungle with the Special Forces "Green Berets"
Survive in the Wilderness with the Canadian and Australian
  Special Forces
Survive at Sea with the U.S. Navy SEALs
Training to Fight with the Parachute Regiment
The World's Best Soldiers

Elite Operations and Training
Escape and Evasion
Surviving Captivity with the U.S. Air Force
Hostage Rescue with the SAS
How to Pass Elite Forces Selection
Learning Mental Endurance with the U.S. Marines

Special Forces Survival Guidebooks
Survival Equipment
Navigation and Signaling
Surviving Natural Disasters
Using Ropes and Knots
Survival First Aid
Trapping, Fishing, and Plant Food
Urban Survival Techniques

NAVIGATION AND SIGNALING

PATRICK WILSON

Introduction by Colonel John T. Carney. Jr., USAF–Ret.
President, Special Operations Warrior Foundation

MASON CREST PUBLISHERS

This edition first published in 2003
by Mason Crest Publishers Inc.
370 Reed Road, Broomall, PA, 19008

Library of Congress Cataloging-in-Publication Data available

ISBN 1-59084-015-1

Editorial and design by
Amber Books Ltd.
Bradley's Close
74–77 White Lion Street
London N1 9PF

Project Editor Chris Stone
Designer Simon Thompson
Picture Research Lisa Wren

Printed and bound in Malaysia

10 9 8 7 6 5 4 3 2 1

ACKNOWLEDGMENT
For authenticating this book, the Publishers would like to thank the Public Affairs Offices of the U.S. Special Operations Command, MacDill AFB, FL.; Army Special Operations Command, Fort Bragg, N.C.; Navy Special Warfare Command, Coronado, CA.; and the Air Force Special Operations Command, Hurlbert Field, FL.

IMPORTANT NOTICE
The survival techniques and information described in this publication are for use in dire circumstances where the safety of the individual is at risk. Accordingly, the publisher cannot accept any responsibility for any prosecution or proceedings brought or instituted against any person or body as a result of the uses or misuses of the techniques and information within.

DEDICATION
This book is dedicated to those who perished in the terrorist attacks of September 11, 2001, and to the Special Forces soldiers who continually serve to defend freedom.

Picture Credits
Corbis: 6, 8, 10, 11, 18, 20, 30, 41, 46, 55, 58; **Marine Picture Library**: 28, 48; **TRH**: 29, 37, 38, 39, 49, 52, 57; **US Dept. of Defense**: 34, 45, 56
Illustrations courtesy of Amber Books and the following supplied by Patrick Mulrey: 14, 16, 22/23, 27, 36, 44, 50
Front cover: **Corbis** (inset), **TRH** (main)

C1369

CONTENTS

INTRODUCTION

Elite forces are the tip of Freedom's spear. These small, special units are universally the first to engage, whether on reconnaissance missions into denied territory for larger, conventional forces or in direct action, surgical operations, preemptive strikes, retaliatory action, and hostage rescues. They lead the way in today's war on terrorism, the war on drugs, the war on transnational unrest, and in humanitarian operations as well as nation building. When large scale warfare erupts, they offer theater commanders a wide variety of unique, unconventional options.

Most such units are regionally oriented, acclimated to the culture and conversant in the languages of the areas where they operate. Since they deploy to those areas regularly, often for combined training exercises with indigenous forces, these elite units also serve as peacetime "global scouts" and "diplomacy multipliers," a beacon of hope for the democratic aspirations of oppressed peoples all over the globe.

Elite forces are truly "quiet professionals": their actions speak louder than words. They are self-motivated, self-confident, versatile, seasoned, mature individuals who rely on teamwork more than daring-do. Unfortunately, theirs is dangerous work. Since "Desert One"—the 1980 attempt to rescue hostages from the U.S. embassy in Tehran, for instance—American special operations forces have suffered casualties in real world operations at close to fifteen times the rate of U.S. conventional forces. By the very nature of the challenges which face special operations forces, training for these elite units has proven even more hazardous.

Thus it's with special pride that I join you in saluting the brave men and women who volunteer to serve in and support these magnificent units and who face such difficult challenges ahead.

Colonel John T. Carney, Jr., USAF–Ret.
President, Special Operations Warrior Foundation

Elite troops in combat need good radio communications with their base, combat aircraft, and with helicopter crews sent out to rescue them.

NAVIGATING WITH A MAP AND A COMPASS

One of the first pieces of training given to those joining the elite forces is navigation. They will also be taught how to signal, since this is vital for attracting the attention of a search aircraft to their position on the ground.

Soldiers setting out on a mission will always thoroughly research the area in advance. They will be equipped with maps of the area and will have spent many hours studying them. The maps will tell them about important land features and will let them work out routes. In addition, elite soldiers will always make a note of the wind direction, the times for sunrise and sunset, and the area's weather patterns. These will all be useful for finding their position. If they are survivors of an accident or on the run from the enemy, they may not have a map, so it is very important to know and learn as much about the **terrain** as possible.

Navigation is not just about reading a map. It also involves being able to read the landscape, determining direction from any visible landmarks, and looking at the land and picturing it as it appears on a map.

However, if elite soldiers have a map, it is important they have one to fit their requirements. For example, it is no use having a map

A map and compass are essential tools that help elite troops to find their bearings more easily.

These American officers plan an operation on Iraqi-held positions on a large wall map during the Gulf War in 1991.

that has a very large scale and shows every detail of the land if they are traveling a distance of over thousands of miles. This may seem obvious, but it is a mistake many people make.

Understanding maps

Maps contain a vast quantity of information. Soldiers do not ignore this immense amount of detail at their fingertips. They learn how to make the most from it. Some of the crucial features, keys, and symbols they need to learn are listed below:

- **Contours**—show the height of the land. The intervals may be in yards, with the approximate value in meters indicated in the margin.
- Scale—gives the **ratio** of map distance to ground distance; for example, 1 inch may equal one mile. Located in the margin.

- **Legend**—explains what the symbols on the map mean. The symbols are not always the same on every map. It is therefore important for the soldier to refer to the legend of whichever map he is using, which is located in the margin.
- **Bar scales**—rulers used to convert map distance to ground distance. Maps usually have three or more bar scales, each a different unit of measurement, such as miles and kilometers. The scales are located in the margin.
- Contour interval—states the height distance between contour lines on the map. This is located in the margin.
- Black **topographic** symbols—point out man-made features, such as roads, buildings, and pipelines. They are also used to show rock features.
- Blue topographic symbols—point out water features, such as lakes, oceans, rivers, and swamps; they also indicate freeways.

Ground troops need to be expert map-readers, as these troops demonstrate while on duty in the Caribbean island of Grenada in 1983.

- Green topographic symbols—point out vegetation, such as woods, forests, and vineyards.
- Brown topographic symbols—show all relief features, like contours.
- Red topographic symbols—show main roads and built-up areas.
- Yellow topographic symbols—show minor roads.

The three norths

The north represented by the grid lines on elite soldiers' maps may differ from the north indicated by their compass.

- True north: the **celestial** north, which is gained from accurate sun readings or from the stars.
- Grid north: the north that map grid lines follow, and from which map bearings are taken.
- Magnetic north: the north to which a **compass** points, and from which all magnetic land bearings are taken.

Soldiers must be of aware of these variations to take accurate bearings. If they have an adjustable compass and know how much it, and their map, differs from true north, they can match them all up to take accurate bearings.

Using maps

The best maps to use are those produced by the U.S. Geographical Survey. Other popular maps are produced by Rand McNally and Hallwag. They are available in a variety of scales, and troops choose the one that best fits their requirements. The most important skill is the ability to translate the lines on a map into the actual shape of the terrain.

Grids

Grids on maps usually form squares to help soldiers assess distances. They can find a position on a map by quoting grid coordinates. The reference is usually given as a six-digit number. To give readings, they always bear in mind that grid references follow the rule "along the corridor, up the stairs." The first three coordinates are taken from the bottom or top margin, the second three numbers from the left or right margin. (Troops must mentally divide each map square into tenths to pinpoint the location.) The map reference for the spot on the map shown is therefore 205558.

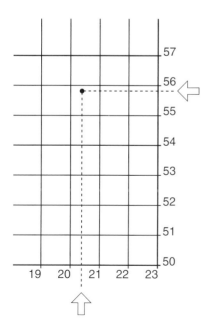

Symbols

A knowledge of map symbols, combined with grids, scale, and distance, give enough information for the soldier to be able to locate two points on a map and work out how long it will take to travel between them.

A map grid, the basic starting point of all map references. Grid references follow the rule "along the corridor and up the stairs."

Contour lines

The differing height of the land is represented on a map by imaginary slices at vertical intervals, called contour lines. By studying these contour lines, elite forces personnel can build up a mental picture of the rise and fall of the land. Starting at sea level, each contour line represents a height above sea level.

Contour lines are usually printed in brown, with every fifth contour being drawn in a heavier line. These heavier lines are called index contours, and somewhere along each one, the line will be broken and its height given. The contour lines between index contours are called intermediate contours.

Using the contour lines on a map, an elite soldier can find the height of any point by:

- Finding the contour interval of the map from the marginal information and noting the amount and unit of measurement.
- Finding the numbered contour line nearest the point of height that is wanted.
- Counting the number of contour lines from the numbered line to the desired point. Multiply this number by the contour interval measurement. Depending on the direction, add or subtract this from the number on the line.

The spacing of contour lines (see opposite) indicates the nature of the slope. Evenly spaced and wide apart lines indicate a gentle, uniform slope (A), while lines evenly spaced and close together indicate a uniform steep slope (B). A vertical or nearly vertical slope is often shown by overlapping contours (C); the lines always points toward the lower ground.

A member of any elite forces unit learns to identify the following terrain features on a map by the shape of their contour lines:

- Hill—a point or small area of high ground. A hill usually slopes down on all sides.
- Valley—level ground, usually with a stream or river running through it, which is bordered on all sides by higher ground. Contours indicating a valley can be U-shaped and run **parallel** to a major stream before crossing it.
- Drainage—a less-developed stream course, in which there is no level ground, making it possible for water to run through the area.

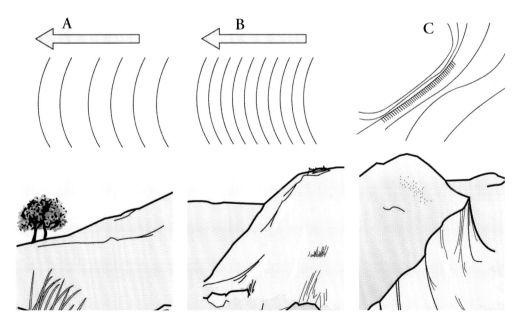

Overhead contour lines provide map-readers with a clear idea of steepness. The closer the lines, the greater the slope of the hill.

The ground slopes upward on each side and toward the head of the drainage. Contours indicating a drainage are V-shaped, with the point of the "V" toward the head of the drainage.
• Depression—resembles a hill, but the contour lines are decreasing in height toward the center of the feature.

Cross section

Members of the elite forces might often want to know a simple cross section of ground between two points. To do this, they will draw on the map a line of the ground they want to see in cross section. Then they will draw a second line, of the same length, horizontally on a

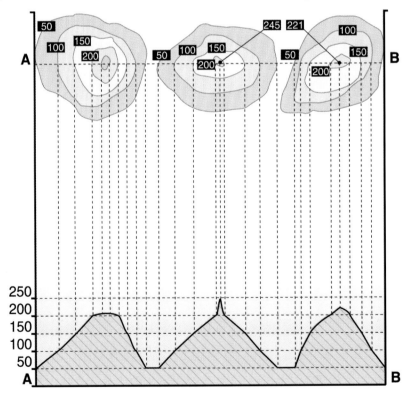

A cross section provides troops with an indication of how the terrain lies between two points. The degree of slope can be seen clearly.

piece of paper to represent ground level (A–B). Then, above and parallel to this ground level, they will draw lines to mark the contour heights—for example, 50, 100, 150, and so on. They mark every point on the map where the line crosses a contour, and transfer this data to their duplicate line on the paper. They raise a **perpendicular** line from each point to mark the appropriate height. They join up all these points to reveal a cross section of the ground.

Bar scales

These are rulers printed on maps, on which distances may be measured as actual ground distances. To the right of zero, the scale is marked in full units of measurement and is called the primary scale. The part to the left of zero is divided into tenths of a unit and is called the extension scale.

Determining straight-line distances on maps

Troops lay a straight-edged piece of paper on the map so the edge of the paper touches both points. Soldiers will mark each point on the paper and move the paper down to the bar scale. They then read the ground distance between the two points.

Marginal notes

These often give the distance from the edge of a map to a town, road, or junction. To measure a road distance from a point on the map to such a point off the map, soldiers will measure the distance to the edge of the map and add the distance specified in the marginal note to that measurement.

Using a compass

Having a compass makes it a great deal easier for elite soldiers to navigate. First they should point the arrow on the front of the compass in the direction they wish to go. Then they should turn the dial so that the "north" mark is in line with the red compass needle. Their bearing will be shown by the black marker, in line with the direction-of-travel marker. Holding the compass in front of him, it is relatively easy to stay on the correct bearing by keeping the north marker on the compass lined up with the compass needle.

To work out their course from a map, elite soldiers will place the side of a compass on a line between their position and their

Taking a compass bearing. Soldiers first point the compass needle in the direction they wish to go and turn the dial so that the north line is in line with the red compass.

MAKING MAPS WITH THE BRITISH SAS

If they do not have a map, the British Special Air Service (SAS) plot their own. All they need is paper, something to write with, and a keen eye. These are guidelines given to troops in training:

- Find the best point to look at the surrounding countryside and examine it closely.
- Note the direction of ridges and count the number you can see.
- Make a general map with blank patches and complete these areas as you gain more information about the area.
- Mark anything of note on the map, such as isolated trees and oddly shaped features.
- Use the map to mark traps and areas where food and fuel can be found.

objective. They will turn the compass dial until the marked **orientating** lines on the dial are parallel with the north–south lines on the map, with the orientating arrow pointing north. Note the reading on the marker line and then add the required number of **mils** for magnetic variation. The compass will now be set on the correct bearing. When the compass is taken off the map, soldiers need only turn their bodies with the compass in front of them, until the red needle lies directly on north. They are then facing idirection they wish to travel.

NAVIGATION WITHOUT A MAP OR A COMPASS

To plan his or her movements in a survival situation, an elite soldier must be able to establish where north, south, east, and west are. This will make it possible to estimate the direction in which the soldier will be traveling and avoid getting lost or walking in circles.

The sun rises in the east and sets in the west. In the northern **hemisphere**, the sun will be due south at its highest point in the sky. In the southern hemisphere, on the other hand, this noonday point will mark due north. The way that shadows move will indicate the hemisphere: clockwise in the north, counterclockwise in the south.

In a survival situation, soldiers can use some simple methods of finding both time and direction (though they all require the sun): by shadow; by the equal shadow method; and by a watch. However, if soldiers are using a watch, it must be one that has minute and hour hands, and not a digital watch. The shadow-tip method is good for spot checks on their journey. (It works at any time during the day when there is sunshine.)

Shadow-tip method

This method can also be used to find the time. The soldier moves the stick to the point where the east–west line and the

If troops do not have a map or compass, they use the sun to navigate. They can use shadows cast by the sun to tell the time.

north–south line meet. He or she then places it vertically in the ground. The west part of the east–west line show 0600 hours and the east part is 1800 hours, regardless of where one is on the planet.

The north–south line now becomes the noon line. The shadow of the stick becomes the hour hand in the shadow clock. The shadow may move either clockwise or counterclockwise, depending on location and the time of year, but this does not alter the manner of reading the shadow clock.

The clock always reads 0600 hours at sunrise and 1800 hours at sunset. Nevertheless, it is a good way of telling time in the absence of a watch.

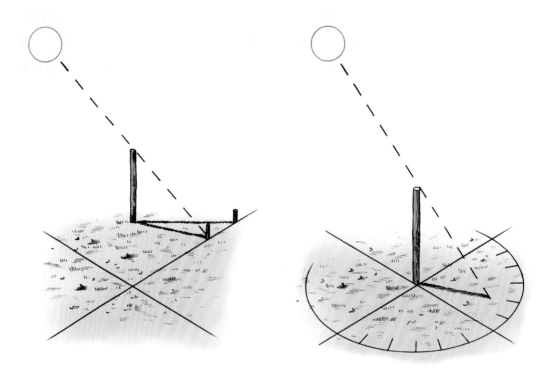

If a soldier does not have a watch, the shadow tip method is an easy way of telling the time. The only object required is a stick.

Equal shadow method

This is more accurate than the shadow-tip method and consequently takes longer to carry out. Soldiers first place a stick vertically into the ground at a level spot to cast a shadow at least one foot (30 cm) long. They mark the first shadow tip in the morning. (It is best to mark a shadow at least 10 minutes before the sun reaches its highest point.)

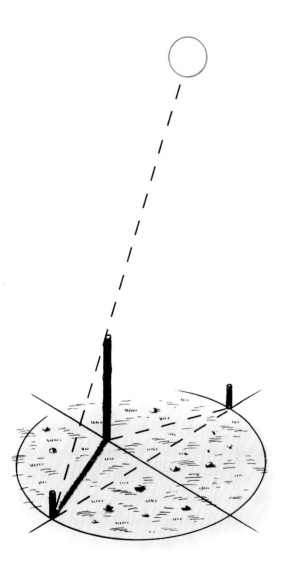

They then draw a clean arc at exactly this distance from the stick, using the stick as the center point. The shadow will shrink and move as midday approaches. After noon, the shadow lengthens and will cross the arc. As it does so, soldiers mark the exact spot where it touches the arc.

Soldiers then draw a straight line through the two marks to obtain and east–west line. (West is the morning mark.) It is

Although it takes longer to carry out, the equal shadow method provides the most accurate time.

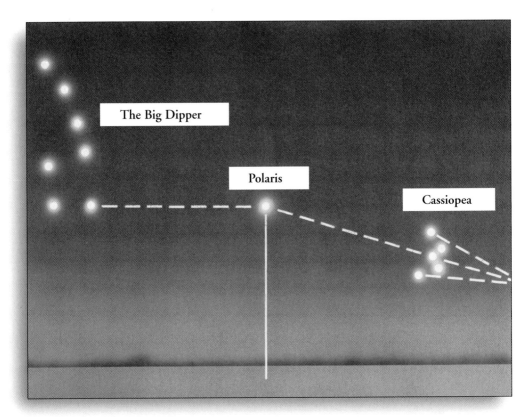

Finding the North Star. The group of stars on the left is called the Big Dipper, and it points to the North Star, also called Polaris.

important for soldiers to remember that they must mark the spot at the time the shadow touches the arc.

The stars

Soldiers are also trained to use stars to find their direction. All elite troops know the following information about the position of the stars:

- Pole Star—in the northern hemisphere it is never more than one degree from the North Celestial Poles (NCP). This is probably one of the most useful stars for working out direction.

- Big Dipper—is very close to the NCP. Its two outer stars point directly to the polestar.
- Cassiopeia—is also very close to the NCP.
- Southern Cross—visible only in the southern hemisphere. An imaginary line through its long axis points toward the South Pole.
- False Cross—a large cross of stars that lies near the Southern Cross.
- True Cross—another name for the Southern Cross.
- Coalsack—the dark region in the sky directly above the South Pole.
- Celestial equator—projection of the Earth's equator into the imaginary celestial sphere. It always intersects the horizon line at the due east and west point of the compass. Thus, any star on the celestial equator rises due east and sets due west.

By making use of the information above, elite soldiers can determine their direction of travel at night, or verify their daytime navigation techniques. The stars that are easily seen on the celestial equator are listed below.

The celestial equator
The following list gives the star groups that lie near the celestial equator and that are visible to the naked eye, together with the month of the year at which each particular star group is on the highest point of its path above the horizon.

January: Eridanus and Taurus.

February: Lepus, Orion, and Monoceros.

March: Canis Minor, Gemini, and Cancer.
April: Sextans and Leo.
May: Cater, Virgo, and Corvus.
June: Bootes.
July: Serpens (Caput), Libra, and Ophiuchus.
August: Serpens (Cauda), Hercules, and Scutum.
September: Aquila and Delphinus.
October: Capricornus, Equuleus, Pegasus, and Aquarius.
November: Pisces.
December: Cetus and Aries.

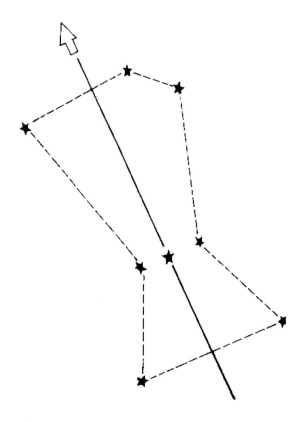

Orion is a good indicator of the direction of north and south.

Orion rises above the equator and can be seen in both hemispheres. It rises on its side, due east, regardless of the observer's position, and sets due west.

In the southern hemisphere, the Southern Cross, a **constellation** of five stars, can be used to determine south, though unfortunately it is not as easy to find as the polestar. To find south, a soldier projects an imaginary line along the cross and four and a half times longer, and then drops it vertically down to the horizon.

Star movement

Star movement can be used to determine a soldier's position. If a star is observed over two fixed points for 15 minutes, it will be seen to move. In the northern hemisphere, the following rules apply:

- If the star is rising, you will be facing due east.
- If the star is falling, you will be facing due west.
- If the star is looping to the right, you will be facing south.
- If the star is looping to the left, you will be facing north.

These rules reverse in the southern hemisphere.

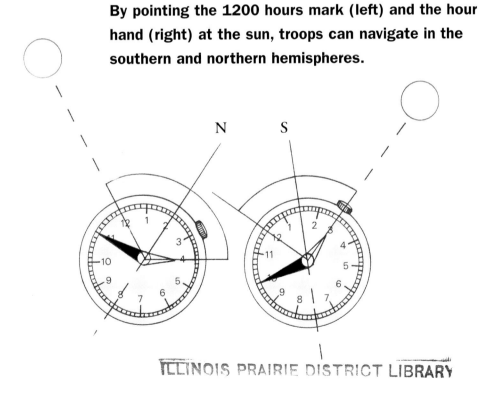

By pointing the 1200 hours mark (left) and the hour hand (right) at the sun, troops can navigate in the southern and northern hemispheres.

A British SAS soldier uses the moon to navigate his way across the desert during the Gulf War in 1991.

The moon

If the moon rises before the sun sets, the illuminated side will be on the west. However, if it rises after the sun sets, the illuminated side will be on the east. If the sun rises at the same time as the sun sets, it will be full and its position in the sky is east at **1800 hours**, southeast at 2100 hours, south at 2359 hours, southwest at 0300 hours, and west at 0600 hours.

Although natural navigation is an important skill to learn, soldiers will always fare better with equipment manufactured for this purpose.

Natural signposts

If elite soldiers cannot see the sun, stars, or the moon due to weather conditions, they will still be able to determine direction by using natural signposts, though these are not as accurate and soldiers need to double check them and treat them with caution. Nevertheless, the following general rules apply:

- Trees—normally grow most of their **foliage** on their sunny side, which in the northern hemisphere is the southern side and in the southern hemisphere the northern side.
- Conifers and willows—usually lean toward their sunny side.

Moss tends to grow on the dark and damp side of trees, where the sun does not shine. This is an important natural signpost.

U.S. MARINE CORPS

The U.S. Marine Corps has a tried-and-tested method for determining location using just a stick and the shadow of the sun.

- They place a stick or branch in the ground at a level spot. They mark the shadow tip with a stone.
- They wait 10 to 20 minutes until the shadow tip moves a few inches. Then they mark the new position of the shadow tip with a stone.
- They draw a straight line through the two marks to obtain an approximate east–west line. (The sun rises in the east and sets in the west; the shadow tip moves in the opposite direction.)
- They draw a line at right angles to the east–west line to get an approximate north–south line.

- Felled trees—their rings are widest on the northern side.
- Moss—tends to favor the dark and damp side of its host.
- Trees with a grainy bark—these usually have a tighter grain on the north-facing side of the trunk.

Dead reckoning

Dead reckoning is a good way of navigating a route from one location to another, though a soldier will need some sort of

DETERMINING DIRECTION WITH A WATCH

If elite soldiers have nondigital watches, they can use them wherever they are to find north and south using the following military method:

- In the northern hemisphere, they must point the hour hand toward the sun.
- A south line can be found midway between the hour hand and 1200 hours. (If in doubt as to which end of the line is north, always remember that the sun is in the east before noon and in the west in the afternoon.)
- In the southern hemisphere, troops point the 1200 hours dial toward the sun. Exactly halfway between the 1200 hours dial and the hour hand will be a north line.
- It is important to set their watches to the true local time.

writing material and paper. The method consists of plotting and recording a series of courses before the journey, each one measured in terms of distance and direction between two points. These courses lead from the starting point to the ultimate destination. The soldier then guesses how long it will take to complete each course. This enables the soldier to determine his or her position at any time by comparing the actual ground position in relation to the plotted course.

To navigate by dead reckoning, elite soldiers need several aids: a map to select their route and for plotting the actual route they take, a compass for direction-finding, a **protractor** for plotting direction and distance on the map, and a route card and log. A route card is used to outline the plan of the proposed journey and the log is used to record the distance they have actually traveled.

Having determined their starting point and plotted their route on the map, soldiers make out their route cards. These describe each leg of the proposed route in terms of distance and direction. When they have completed their route card, they are ready to move.

It is important that, when walking, they carefully record each course taken and the distance covered on each one. This record is the soldiers' log. Memory is not enough. If they have to change from their route because of terrain, they must record these adjustments in the log.

When using dead reckoning, it is important the soldiers establish the length of their average pace. However, while remembering the average pace, the elite forces soldier will always remember to take into account the following:

- Slopes—the pace lengthens on a downward slope and shortens on an upward slope, though not too much on very gentle slopes.
- Winds—a headwind shortens the pace and a tailwind increases it.
- Surfaces—gravel, mud, sand, long grass, deep snow, and similar surface materials tend to shorten the pace.
- Elements—snow, rain, and ice all reduce the length of the pace.
- Clothing—carrying excess weight of clothing shortens the pace of a soldier and shoe type can affect traction and thus pace length.

SIGNALING

An elite soldier must be able to give signals that a rescue team, specifically an aircraft, will be able to see clearly. A radio and flares are recognized as the best ways to alert a rescue aircraft. If the soldier has neither of these, then smoke or fire is the next best alternative. Three fires or three columns of smoke are internationally recognized distress signals.

Manufactured signals

If soldiers have come down in an aircraft, or they are stranded in a life raft, they may have access to a signaling system designed for that purpose. On a mission, they will always equip themselves with some of the items listed below:

• Transceiver—can transmit tone or voice and will receive tone or voice.
• Beacon—can only transmit tone.
• Radio—survival radios are generally line-of-sight communication devices, thus the best transmission range will be obtained when they are operating from clear, unobstructed terrain.
• Hand-held flares—day flares produce a bright-colored smoke; night flares are very bright and can be seen over long distances.
• Hand-held launched flares—designed to overcome the problems of terrain masking and climatic conditions.

Radios are among the best means of alerting aircraft and communicating with other soldiers.

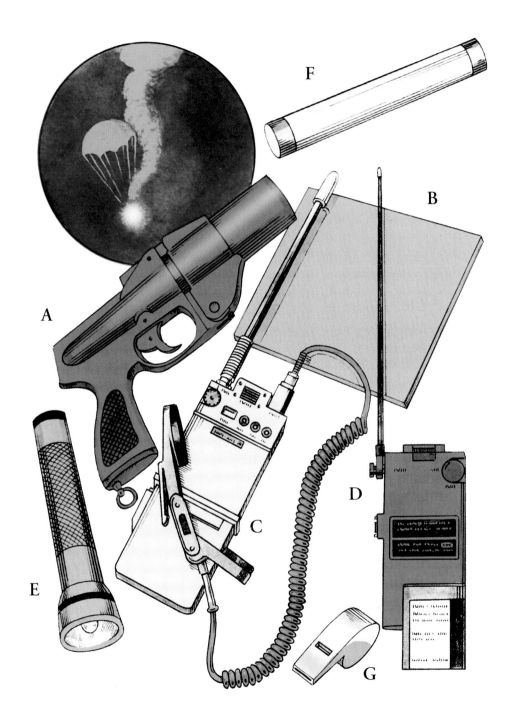

Communication equipment including (A) a flare gun, (B) mirror, (C) radio, (D) transceiver, (E) flashlight, (F) hand-held flare, and (G) a whistle.

- Tracer ammunition—if available, can be used for signaling. When fired, the round appears as an orange-red flash. The soldier takes care not to direct it at a rescue aircraft.
- Sea marker—a powder that stains the sea green or orange.
- Paulin signals—rubberized nylon markers that are blue on one side and yellow on the other.
- Whistle—useful for short-range signaling.
- Light signals—flashlights or strobe lights that can be seen over great distances.
- Signal mirror—a mirror flash can be visible up to a range of 100 miles (60 km) in ideal conditions.

A mirror glinting off the sun can be easily spotted by overhead aircraft. It is often used as a signaling device during secret missions.

This Israeli soldier wears an S10 respirator during hostage-rescue training. The respirator protects him from breathing in the smoke.

Smoke

In daylight, smoke will be recognizable over long distances. Elite soldiers will build, cover, and maintain a signal fire ready to be lit at a moment's notice. They will always try to create smoke that will contrast with the background terrain. If they put green leaves, moss, or damp wood on a fire, they will get white smoke; rubber or oil-soaked rags on a fire will produce black smoke.

Fire

This is very effective for signaling at night. Soldiers will build a fire that gives out a lot of light. A burning tree is a good way of attracting attention. **Pitch-bearing trees** can be set on fire when green. For other types of trees, soldiers will place dry wood in the lower branches, and set it on fire. The flames will ignite the tree foliage. They are trained always to remember to select a tree apart from other trees—they do not want to start a forest fire!

Reflector

On a sunny day, mirrors, polished canteen cups, belt buckles, or other objects will reflect the sun's rays. A soldier will have practiced signaling many times. Mirror signals can be seen for 62 miles (100 km) under normal conditions and more than 100 miles (160 km) in a desert environment.

A stranded soldier's best chance of being rescued by comrades is by staying in close radio contact.

Ground-to-air signals

There are several factors elite soldiers must take into account with regard to ground-to-air signals if they are to be effective and help the soldiers get rescued. Above all, they must try to visualize what their signals will look like when viewed by a pilot from the air.

- Size: signals should be as large as possible. Remember, they have to be seen from the air.
- Ratio: signals should be in proportion, especially if the soldier is laying out letters. They must be seen clearly from the air.
- Angularity: a soldier makes all pattern signals with straight lines and square corners because there are no straight lines or square corners in nature. This makes it obvious that it is a man-made signal.

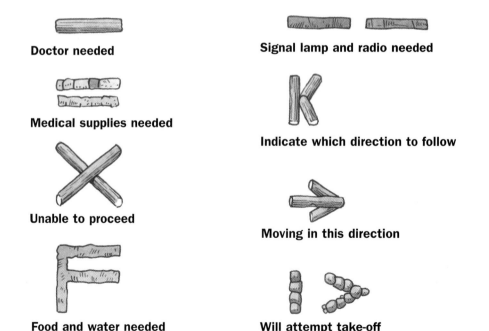

Doctor needed

Signal lamp and radio needed

Medical supplies needed

Unable to proceed

Indicate which direction to follow

Moving in this direction

Food and water needed

Will attempt take-off

Ground-to-air signals must be made visible to rescue pilots. Some common ground-to-air signals and their meanings are shown above.

Troops should signal and use communication equipment in clear terrain. In wooded or enclosed areas, signals can become blocked.

- Contrast: the signal should stand out against the background.
- On snow: any dye used around the signal will add contrast.
- On grass: burn the grass to make a pattern.
- Orange material: tends to blend in, not stand out, when placed on a green or brown background.
- Outlines: outline a signal with green tree boughs, brush, or rocks to produce shadows.
- Location: a signal should be placed where it can be seen from all directions. (A large, open area is best.)
- Meaning: a signal should tell the rescue service something about the overall situation.

Emergency signals

Signals signifying a person in distress are recognized by the military all over the world. Soldiers know them by heart. When laying them out they make them as large as possible, at least 40 feet (12 m) long and 10 feet (3 m) wide. At night, soldiers will dig or scrape a signal in the earth, snow, or sand, then pour gasoline into it and ignite it.

A .—	M — —	Y —.— —
B —...	N —.	Z — —.. —
C —.—.	O — — —	1 .— — — —
D —..	P .— —.	2 ..— —
E .	Q — —.—	3 ...— —
F ..—.	R .—.	4 ....—
G — —.	S ...	5 .....
H	T —	6 —....
I ..	U ..—	7 — —...
J .— — —	V ...—	8 — — —..
K —.—	W .— —	9 — — — —.
L .—..	X —..—	0 — — — — —

In Morse code, each sequence of dots and dashes stands for a letter of the alphabet. Once learned, troops can send messages.

This signal will be visible not only at night, but also during the day where the ground has been burned.

Troops must destroy all ground-to-air symbols after rescue, otherwise they will go on marking after they have gone. Failure to do so may result in other aircraft spotting them and attempting a rescue.

Morse code

Troops can transmit messages using Morse code by flashing lights on and off, using reflectors, using sound, or by waving a flag or a shirt tied to a stick. (For a "dot" they swing to the right and make a figure-eight, for a "dash" they swing to the left and make a figure-eight).

Body signals

This series of signals from a person in distress on the ground will be understood by an aircrew. It is advisable for soldiers to use a cloth in the hand to emphasize the Yes and No signals. It is important for elite soldiers to be aware of the different meanings given by changing from frontal to sideways positions and the use of the legs. Whenever they are making signals, soldiers always do so in a clear and exaggerated way. (It is easy to forget that they will be a great distance from the aircraft.)

An aircraft that has understood your message will tilt its wings up and down in daylight or make green flashes with its signal lights at night. If the pilot has not understood the soldier's message, he will circle his aircraft during daylight or make red flashes with his signal lights at night. Once a pilot has received and understood the

If troops do not have anything to make ground signals with, they may choose to use body signals to attract the attention of aircraft.

soldier's first message, it is then possible for the soldier to transmit another message. The soldier needs to be patient. It takes time, but an elite soldier will try not to confuse the pilot.

Shadow signals

Shadow signals can be very effective for signaling, though elite soldiers must construct them in the proper way. They need to make sure they build them in a large enough clearing and that their signals contrast with their immediate surroundings. Troops follow these guidelines when making shadow signals in the following terrain:

- Arctic winter—build a snowblock wall, and line the blocks alongside the trench from which the blocks were cut.
- Arctic summer—construct walls from stones, turf, or wood.
- Winter below the snowline—stick green boughs in the snow and build a wall of brush and boughs around them.
- Summer below the treeline—use piles of rocks, dead wood, logs, and blocks of turf cut out from the earth.

Mountain rescue code

The codes listed below are internationally recognized mountain rescue signals. Troops learn them and practice transmitting

Troops using a global positioning system (GPS) to find their location. Navigation equipment is becoming increasingly sophisticated.

them. (They should always carry something to enable them to transmit a signal.)

SOS

To send, they use the following flare, sound, and light signals:

- Flare—red.
- Sound—three short blasts, three long blasts, three short blasts. (They repeat after a one-minute interval.)
- Light—three short flashes, three long flashes, three short flashes. (They repeat after a one-minute interval.)

Help needed

To send, they use the following flare, sound, and light signals:

- Flare—red.

Hand-held flares produce a brightly colored smoke. They can be seen by rescue craft from a distance of up to five miles (8 km).

- Sound—six blasts in quick succession. (They repeat after a one-minute interval.)
- Light—six flashes in quick succession. (They repeat after a one-minute interval.)

Message understood

To send, they use the following flare, sound, and light signals:

- Flare—white.
- Sound—three blasts in quick succession. (They repeat after a one-minute interval.)

SIGNAL FIRES

Fire is not only useful for heat and cooking in a survival situation. It can also be used for signaling. Learn these British SAS tips about where to build signal fires. It is important to get it right the first time—there might not be a second chance!

- Keep green boughs, oil, or rubber close by to create smoke.
- Build earth wells around fires if surrounded by vegetation or trees.
- Build fires in clearings. Do not build among trees: the canopy will block out the signal.
- If by a river or lake, build rafts on which to place fires and tie them in position.

Troops are often dropped behind enemy lines. It is essential they carry communication equipment so they can pass messages back to base.

- Light: three flashes in quick succession. (They repeat after a one-minute interval.)

Return to base

To send this signal, they use the following flare, sound, and light signals:

- Flare—green.
- Sound—prolonged succession of blasts.
- Light—prolonged succession of flashes.

Information signals

Soldiers will use information signals when they leave the scene of a crash or abandon camp. They always leave a large arrow to indicate the direction in which they have set off. All their trails thereafter should be marked (unless their mission is secret).

Rescue

Once the rescue services have established the position of a survivor, a rescue operation will be launched. On land, this will usually

A helicopter rescue during the Vietnam War. Signaling from troops on the ground must be effective to attract a pilot in jungle terrain.

be in the form of an aircraft or helicopter, and a ship or boat if you are in the water. Troops are trained to be aware of the effects of weather and terrain on the rescue aircraft. They are taught to try to avoid overhangs, cliffs, or the sides of steep slopes if possible.

Helicopter rescue

Helicopters will make a rescue by landing or hovering. Landings are usually necessary on high ground, where a helicopter has insufficient power for hovering. **Hoist** recovery is the preferred method. If a helicopter has to land to pick up soldiers, they will not approach it from the rear, because this is a blind spot for the crew and the tail rotor is unprotected. Similarly, soldiers will be careful of being hit by the rotors if they are approaching the helicopter down a slope. Troops must be aware of any materials on the ground that may be sucked into the rotor blades, such as a parachute or tent. Where possible, troops pick them up before the helicopter lands.

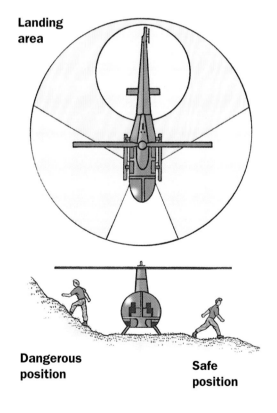

Landing area

Dangerous position

Safe position

Helicopters require an area of 82 feet (25 m) to land safely.

A soldier will always try to mark the landing site with a large "H," at least 10 feet (3 m) high, and will make sure the materials are securely anchored to the ground.

If troops are in sandy terrain, they will try to water the sand to keep dust down. In snow, they will try to compact the surface down as much as possible. (Soft, wet snow will cling to the aircraft, and powdery snow will swirl and restrict the pilot's vision.)

If soldiers are being **winched** aboard a hovering helicopter, they let the cable touch the ground before touching it. (All aircraft build up a lot of static electricity, and they may receive a shock if they grab it before it discharges through the earth.) They then fit themselves into the strop and give the "thumbs up" sign. They are trained to never make any further signals, especially raising their arms—they could slip out of the strap.

When they get to the cabin door, soldiers let the winch man do everything and obey him to the letter (even if they have experience of traveling by helicopter). Once they are out of the winch, they will be told to sit down and shown where to sit. In the helicopter, they must obey the aircrew at all times.

Aircraft rescue

If an aircraft is able to land to pick them up, soldiers will not approach it until it has come to a halt and the pilot or another member of the crew has signaled them to do so.

Once rescued, the soldier should, where relevant, inform the rescue services at once of any survivors that have become separated from the group.

NAVIGATION IN HOSTILE CLIMATES

Troops are all too aware that getting lost in a hostile climate may lead to death. Good navigation is essential, and troops are provided with a lot of training before joining the elite forces.

Desert

Traveling in the desert can be extremely hazardous. An elite soldier must consider the effect, the weather, and the amount of food and water required, will have on the ability to travel. He or she does not underestimate the climate or the terrain. In daytime, the scorching heat will make movement **impractical**. However, if troops are traveling at night in rocky or mountainous deserts, they have to be careful to avoid dangers such as canyons, which could result in them falling and getting seriously injured.

At night, elite soldiers use the stars and the moon to navigate. During the day, they can use a compass or landmarks. However, they will be aware that in the desert, because of the glare of the sun and lack of landmarks, distances are difficult to estimate and objects difficult to size. Troops try to follow animal trails and hope they lead to rivers or watering holes. The wind can also be used as a direction indicator. However, soldiers are aware that sandstorms can totally mislead and confuse a person. When the storm is over,

Troops from the British Mountain and Arctic Warfare Cadre make their way through hazardous terrain in Norway in 1995.

DESERT TRAVEL RULES

Traveling during the day in the desert can be a killer. U.S. Marine Corps regulations are strict concerning movement in desert regions.

- Avoid the midday sun: travel only in the evening, at night, or in the early morning.
- Do not walk aimlessly: try to head for the coast, a road, a path, a water source, or an inhabited location; try to follow trails.
- Avoid loose sand and rough terrain: they will cause fatigue.
- In sandstorms, lie on your side with your back to the wind, then cover your face and sleep through the storm. (Don't worry—you won't get buried.)
- Seek shelter on the leeward side of hills.
- Objects always appear closer than they really are in the desert. Therefore, multiply all your distance estimations by three.

all the landmarks they were using may have disappeared. Therefore, soldiers must mark their route before a storm so that they can pick up the trail afterward. Placing a stick to indicate direction is sufficient.

Mirages can also play havoc with a person's navigation. Soldiers must be especially alert for mirages concealing objects, creating imaginary objects, and making red objects seem closer and larger. Mirages are common during the heat of the day.

Polar regions

Due to the harshness of the terrain, movement in polar regions is very dangerous. Military operations in snow and ice areas can be very difficult, largely due to the unpredictable weather. Signaling and navigation can be very hard. The U.S. Army has drawn up the following guidelines to help its troops:

- "**Whiteouts**" (complete snow cover and extremely thick cloud cover) can result in troops falling into crevasses, over cliffs or high snow ridges, and losing direction.

Communicating in the desert. The soldier on the left speaks to base camp while his comrade keeps watch for enemy artillery (weapons).

- A compass is absolutely vital, but because of magnetic variation, navigating a true course is difficult.
- In summer, there will be a mass of bogs and swamps, which are all difficult to cross. These are home to a mass of mosquitoes, which can inflict severe discomfort if body parts are not covered. Troops should always use insect repellent.
- In mountainous terrain, soldiers may fall into crevasses and glacial streams. Troops use a stick to probe ahead.
- In timbered areas, travel will be easier on skies or snowshoes during the cold months.

Canadian Air Force pilots operate over hostile terrain in the north of their country. They must be experienced in ice travel and navigation skills if they have to bale out of their planes. In the summer, they

These U.S. 10th Mountain Division troops stay close to each other when navigating mountainous terrain so that they do not get lost.

Soldiers from the British Marines Mountain and Arctic Warfare Cadre travel on a motorized snowmobile during training in Norway.

avoid dense vegetation, rough terrain, insects, soft ground, swamps, and lakes. They cross glacier-fed streams in the early morning to avoid raging torrents, which are sparked by rising temperatures. They travel on ridges and game trails.

In the winter, they do not move in a blizzard or during extremely cold weather. It is better for them to camp and save their strength. They are also very careful of thin ice, heavy snow, and air pockets if traveling on frozen rivers. They are taught always to use a pole to test the ground ahead.

When walking in polar regions, troops should protect their whole body from the cold and wind, especially the head and feet. By keeping active, they will keep blood **circulating** in their body.

However, they try to avoid sweating. If they start to overheat, they loosen or remove some of their clothing. Goggles are vital to stop troops from getting snow-blindness. Troops also learn to protect their fingers. They always keep their hands covered and never place their bare hands on metal when it is extremely cold. If soldiers' hands get very cold, they place them inside their clothing under their armpits or next to their stomach. Clenching and unclenching their hands in mittens also helps keep them warm.

Because compasses are unreliable near the poles, troops also learn to use the stars at night and the shadow-tip method during the day. In addition, they need to choose their route carefully at the start of the day, since the last thing they need is to get cold and wet traveling through swamps and bogs. Where possible, they try to follow a waterway: most settlements are situated on a river or stream. If they

With a global positioning system (GPS), these US Army troops can pin-point their location anywhere on the planet.

follow a waterway, they will be able to replace the fluids they lose by walking. There will also be fish in the rivers or streams, and animals are also attracted to the area, which gives troops the opportunity of catching them. In addition, there will probably be an abundance of edible plants growing alongside it.

When following a waterway, troops resist the temptation to build a raft and float on it unless the river flows gently. Many rivers are fast, cold, and dangerous and can smash a raft into splinters. The chances are that the troops will not know the river and even if it appears calm, there may be rocks under the water that could tear the raft to pieces in seconds. Troops remember the following points when navigating in snow and ice areas:

- Poor or nonexistent roads mean they are of little use for cross-country navigation.
- In winter, long nights, blowing snows, and fog limit visibility.
- Snowfalls can cover up tracks and landmarks, and therefore make it easier to make navigation mistakes.
- There is limited daylight in the winter.
- There may be a multitude of lakes, ponds, and creeks that are not on the map. This can be confusing and may also lengthen travel times.

For signaling in polar regions, troops always carry a reflector in a handy place in case an aircraft appears. Alternatively, they carry fire-starting material in their pockets so that they are ready to start a fire. They know that speed is vital. They may have only one chance and do not want to ruin it by being unprepared.

GLOSSARY

Bar scales Used to convert map distance to ground distance.

Celestial Meaning "of the sky."

Circulating Flowing around.

Compass Instrument for determining direction using a magnetic needle.

Constellation A collection or group of stars.

Contours Indicates the height of land.

Foliage Leaves and vegetation.

Gradient A slope. A severe gradient would be a steep slope.

Hemisphere The world is split into two of these, the northern and southern hemisphere. The equator is the line that divides the two.

Hoist To lift.

Impractical Something that is difficult to do or cannot be done.

Leeward The direction in which the wind is blowing.

Legend In navigation this is the explanation of map symbols.

Mil(s) A thousandth of an inch.

Mirage An illusion, normally of water, caused by heat.

Navigation The finding of position and the direction of one's course.

Orientating Working out one's position.

Parallel Running alongside without intersecting.

Perpendicular Used in measurements. Meaning straight up and down.

Pitch-bearing trees Trees that have a lot of resin (a flammable substance).

Protractor Instrument that works out angles.

Ratio The relationship between two numbers.

SOS Call for help in an emergency, meaning Save Our Souls.

Terrain Land.

Topographic Relating to features of the landscape. Topography is the study of landscapes.

Whiteout Extreme snow and/or cloud cover where visibility is extremely limited.

Winched Lifted using a winch (the crank of a wheel or an axle).

1800 hours To avoid confusion, the army measures time according to the 24-hour clock, so 1800 hours is 6 P.M.

EQUIPMENT REQUIREMENTS

Clothing and shelter
Thermal underwear
Thin layer of synthetic material
Woolen or wool mixture shirt
Woven fiber sweater or jacket (normally a fleece)
Waterproof and windproof final layer
Two pairs of socks (minimum)
Compact, light, windproof pants with numerous pockets with zippers, to carry items securely
Waterproof pants
Gloves—leather or mittens
Balaclava (a tight woolen garment covering the head and neck)
Spare clothing—socks, underwear, shirts, etc.
Soft, well-maintained leather boots
H-frame bergen (backpack) with side pockets
Portable, lightweight, waterproof shelter

Survival tin
A knife
Matches
Flint
Sewing kit
Water purification tablets
Compass
Mirror
Safety pins
Wire
Plastic bag
Antiseptic cream
Snare wire

Survival bag
Pliers with wire cutter
Dental floss (for sewing)
Folding knife
Ring saw
Snow shovel
Signal cloth
Fishing hooks and flies
Weights and line
Multivitamins
Protein tablets
Large chocolate bar
Dried eggs
Dried milk
File

Cutlery set
Three space blankets
Four candles
Microlite flashlight
Extra battery and bulb
Fire starter
Windproof and waterproof matches
Butane lighter
Insect repellent
Snares
Plastic cup
Slingshot and ammunition
Knife sharpener
Whistle
Soap
Two orange smoke signals
Mess tin

EQUIPMENT FOR HOSTILE TERRAIN

Desert
Light-colored clothing (reflects
  sunlight)

Cloth neckpiece
Sunglasses or goggles

Tropical regions
Talcum powder
Insect repellent
Machete
Hammock
Mosquito netting
Tropical medicines

Polar regions
Waterproof and windproof outer
  layers
Many inner layers of clothing for
insulation
Goggles
Three layers of socks
Waterproof canvas boots
Ice axe
Ski stick
Rope

USEFUL WEBSITES

http://www.rin.org.uk
http://www.ion.org
http://www.colorado.Edu/geography/gcraft/notes/gps/gps_f.html
http://www.uscg.mil/vtm/pages/rules.htm
http://www.pbs.org/wgbh/nova/longitudes/gpsgame.html
http://www.princeton.edu/oa/manual/mapcompass.shtml
http://www.artrans.com/rmsg/trans/mapsmap.htm

FURTHER READING

Boga, Steve. *Orienteering*. Mechanisburg, Pa.: Stackpole Books, 1997.

Burns, Bob. *Wilderness Navigation: Finding Your Way Using Map, Compass, Altimeter, and GPS*. Seattle, Wash.: Mountaineers Books, 1999.

Department of Defense. *Map Reading and Land Navigation*. New York: Apple Pie Publishers, 1999.

Jacobsen, Cliff. *Basic Essentials: Map and Compass*. Guilford, Conn.: Globe Pequot, 1999.

Kjellstrom, Bjorn. *Be Expert with Map and Compass*. Palo Alto, Calif.: Hungry Minds, 1994.

Letham, Lawrence. *GPS Made Easy: Using Global Positioning Systems in the Outdoors*. Seattle, Wash.: Mountaineers Books, 2001.

Navigation Rules: Rules of the Road. Arcata, Calif.: Paradise Cay Publications, 2000.

ABOUT THE AUTHOR

Patrick Wilson was educated at Marlborough College, Wiltshire and studied history at Manchester University. He was a member of the Officer Training Corps, and for the past seven years he has been heavily involved in training young people in the art of survival on Combined Cadet Force (CCF) and Duke of Edinburgh Courses. He has taught history at St. Edward's School, Oxford, Millfield School, and currently at Bradfield College in England.

His main passion is military history. His first book was *Dunkirk—From Disaster to Deliverance* (Pen & Sword, 2000). Since then he has written *The War Behind the Wire* (Pen & Sword, 2000), which accompanied a television documentary on prisoners of war. He recently edited the diaries of an Australian teenager in the First World War.

INDEX

References in italics refer to illustrations